REACH FOR THE STARS

A Children's History Book of Visionaries and Their Dreams

KEN DEAN

Illustrated by Mayra Espinoza

Copyright by Kenneth W. Dean
Reach for the Stars

All rights reserved. In accordance with the U.S. Copyright Act of 1976, the canning, uploading and electronic sharing of any part of this book without the permission of the publisher is unlawful piracy and theft of the author's intellectual property. If you would like to use material from this book (other than for review purposes), prior written permission must be obtained by contacting the publisher at **info@knowledgepowerinc.com**. Thank you for your support of the author's rights.

ISBN: 978-1-7322665-3-7

Library of Congress Control Number: 2019933577

Edited by: Laurel J. Davis
Cover Design: Angie Alaya
Interior Designer: Amit Dey
Literary Director: Sandra L. Slayton

Published by:

KP Publishing Company
A Division of Knowledge Power Communications, Inc.
Valencia, CA 91355
www.kp-pub.com

Printed in the United States of America

Dedication

This book is dedicated to all those who have dreams.

*All the people you will read about
in this book had a dream.
They reached for the stars to make
their dreams come true.
You too, can make your dreams come true.
If only you reach for the stars,
for your goals, ideas, and dreams.
Remember that nothing is out of reach
or impossible if you believe in your dreams and*

REACH FOR THE STARS!

Ken Dean

Table of Contents

Dedication v
Dr. Martin Luther King, Jr. 5
John F. Kennedy 7
Thomas Alva Edison 9
Alexander Graham Bell 11
Mother Teresa 13
César Chávez 15
Robert F. Kennedy 17
Abraham Lincoln 19
Sir Winston Churchill 21
Jackie Robinson 23
Thomas Jefferson 25
General Douglas MacArthur 27
Franklin D. Roosevelt 29
George Washington 31
Ronald Reagan 33
Albert Einstein 35
Benjamin Franklin 37
Mohandas Gandhi 39
My Dream 41
About the Author 43

MARTIN LUTHER KING
1929~1968
CIVIL RIGHTS LEADER

Dr. Martin Luther King, Jr.

(1929-1968)
Minister, Civil Rights Activist

Dr. Martin Luther King, Jr. had a dream that all men are created equal. He began his work on this vision in 1955 by starting a boycott against "whites only" sections on public buses in Montgomery, Alabama.

He was born Michael King, Jr. on January 15, 1929. His father had adopted the name of Martin Luther King, Sr. in honor of Martin Luther, who was a German protestant religious leader. Later, young Michael would also adopt the name Martin.

Like his father, Dr. King was ordained a Baptist minister at age 19. He skipped both the ninth and eleventh grades. At the age of 15, in 1944, he entered Morehouse College in Atlanta, Georgia, and received a Bachelor of Arts degree in sociology. In 1948, Dr. King was very popular in school and was elected valedictorian of his class at Crozer Theological Seminary near Chester, Pennsylvania, in 1951, with a Bachelor of Divinity degree. He received his Ph.D. from Boston University in Boston, Massachusetts, in 1955.

Dr. King's historic, ground-breaking speech, "I Have a Dream," was delivered on August 28, 1963, to 250,000 supporters at the Lincoln Memorial in Washington, D.C.

Dr. King was awarded the Nobel Peace Prize on October 14, 1964, for his nonviolent resistance to racial prejudice in America. At just 35 years old, he was the youngest person ever to receive the award.

Some of Dr. King's famous quotes are:

"I've seen the promised land." ((Part of a speech he gave the night before his death.)

"Whenever men and women straighten their backs up, they're going somewhere, because a man can't ride your back unless it's bent."

Dr. King's words, "From every mountainside, let freedom ring," have as much importance to this day as the day he uttered them. These words should live forever for all nations and all people.

On April 4, 1968, Dr. Martin Luther King, Jr. was assassinated in Memphis, Tennessee.

John F. Kennedy

(1917-1963)
35th United States President

John Fitzgerald Kennedy's dream was to keep America and its people safe, along with the dream for America to one day reach the moon. He did not live long enough to see this dream come true.

At age 43 in 1961, after serving in both the United States Congress and the United States Senate, Mr. Kennedy was the second youngest man and the first Roman Catholic to be elected as a United States President.

During World War II, Mr. Kennedy was a war hero and was awarded the Purple Heart. In 1957, he won the Pulitzer Prize for his wonderful novel, *Profiles in Courage*.

President Kennedy faced down the Russians during the Cuban Missile Crisis in October 1962, an event the whole world watched in which the Russians had their missiles in Cuba pointed at the United States. This led to the 1963 Treaty with Russia on banning nuclear testing.

The Kennedy family were very wealthy and prominent Irish Catholics from Boston, Massachusetts. President Kennedy's father was a successful banker and made fortunes in the stock market.

To most people, President Kennedy was known as "Jack." Blessed with a captivating and radiant smile, he was quite handsome and very charming. While at Harvard University, he was incredibly popular with his classmates.

Some of President Kennedy's famous quotes are:

"Let us never negotiate out of fear but let us never fear to negotiate."

"Liberty without learning is always in peril; learning without liberty is always in vain."

"A man may die, nations may rise and fall, but an idea lives on."

On November 22, 1963, President Robert F. Kennedy was assassinated in Dallas, Texas, at the young age of 46, in front of the world.

John F. Kennedy Library and Museum

REACH FOR THE STARS

"I WANT TO SEE A PHOTOGRAPH IN EVERY AMERICAN HOME."

THOMAS ALVA EDISON
1847~1931
SCIENTIST AND INVENTOR

Thomas Alva Edison

(1847-1931)

Inventor and Businessman

Through his dreams and hard work, Thomas Edison invented the light bulb, which gave us the light we have today and brought lighting to the world.

In 1880, he was granted a patent for the light bulb through his Edison Illuminate Company, which later became General Electric Corporation, one of the largest companies in the world today.

Mr. Edison also invented the phonograph. The words first recorded on a phonograph were, "Mary had a little lamb." One of his major inventions was the motion picture taken by a camera called a kinetograph.

Early in Mr. Edison's life, he was affected with scarlet fever, which left him with hearing difficulties in both ears that eventually left him nearly deaf.

Although Mr. Edison was taught arithmetic, reading, and writing by his mother, who was a schoolteacher, he taught himself much by reading on his own.

Mr. Edison's first invention, at only 22 years of age, was an improved stock ticker. He was paid $40,000 for the rights, which at the time was a huge amount of money. Another invention brought him $100,000 for two signals going in two different directions at the same time.

As a clever businessman, Mr. Edison held more than 1,000 patents for his many inventions. By the 1870s, he had a reputation as a first-time inventor.

Mr. Edison had all kinds of dreams and visions, one of which was that he wanted to install a large speaker inside the Statue of Liberty so "she could talk" to the people visiting her.

He was famous for many quotes, some of which are:

"Opportunity is missed by most people because it is dressed in overalls and looks like work."

"I have not failed, I just found 10,000 ways that won't work."

"Genius is one percent inspiration and 99 percent perspiration."

Mr. Edison worked on projects such as submarine detectors and gun-location techniques. He was against violence and was quoted as saying, "I am proud of the fact that I have never invented weapons to kill."

Alexander Graham Bell

(1847-1922)
Scientist and Inventor

Like Thomas Edison, Alexander Graham Bell had a dream and a passion for shaping the future.

In 1876, at the age of 29, Mr. Bell invented the telephone. Just one year later he started his own company, Bell Telephone Company.

Today, all over the world, just about everyone has a phone. From "land lines" to cell phones, and it all started with Mr. Bell.

Mr. Bell personally held 18 patents on his inventions and 12 more he shared with other inventors.

Mr. Bell's mother was a skilled pianist, even though she was deaf. Like Edison, he was home schooled by his mother, who maintained a significant influence on him right into his adult life.

At age 16, Mr. Bell accepted a position to teach elocution (the art of public speaking) at Weston House Academy in Scotland. His father and grandfather were authorities on elocution and speech correction. This started Mr. Bell's road to inventing the telephone when, in the 1870s, he set up a workshop to study the human voice.

Between 1873 and 1874, Mr. Bell started to work on transmitting the human voice over wires with the assistance of a skilled electrician by the name of Thomas Watson, who knew how to develop the instruments Bell needed.

The first telephone call was when Mr. Watson heard Mr. Bell's voice through the wire. When Mr. Bell demonstrated the telephone to the Emperor of Brazil, the emperor said, "My God, it talks!"

During the years from 1866 to 1886, more than 150,000 people in America owned a telephone.

A famous saying by Alexander Graham Bell was:

"When one door closes, another door opens; but we so often look so long and so regretfully upon the closed door, that we do not see the ones which open for us."

Mother Teresa

(1910-1997)
Saint

Mother Teresa's dream even as a child was that she was meant to help those in need, and she would accompany her mother on missions of mercy.

In 1919, when Mother Teresa was eight years old, her father suddenly became ill and died. At this time, Mother Teresa became extraordinarily close to her mother, establishing a strong bond.

In 1928, at the age of 18, Mother Theresa left her home in Skopje, Yugoslavia to join a convent in Calcutta, India, to become a nun. From there she became a missionary and a peacemaker. Sadly, she would never see her mother and sister again.

Her mother told her, "My child, never eat a single mouthful unless you are sharing it with others." She also told her, "When you do good, do it quietly."

Mother Teresa was a Roman Catholic nun who became famous for her dream to help the poor, the starving, and the destitute, which she did by living among them herself. However, during her first year with no money, she resorted to begging for food and supplies.

At the time of her death, Mother Teresa had formed Missionaries of Charity which operated all over the world with 610 missions in 123 countries, including Russia, Cuba, and China.

Some of Mother Teresa's wonderful quotes are:

"God doesn't require us to succeed; He only requires that you try."

"If you judge people, you have no time to love them."

"Kind words can be short and easy to speak, but their echoes are truly endless."

"One of the greatest diseases is to be nobody to anybody."

"Being unwanted, unloved, uncared for, forgotten by everybody, I think that is a much greater hunger, a much greater poverty than the person who has nothing to eat."

REACH FOR THE STARS

"NON-VIOLENCE REALLY REST ON THE RESERVOIR THAT YOU HAVE TO CREATE IN YOURSELF OF PATIENCE."

CESAR CHAVEZ
1927~1993
CIVIL RIGHTS AND LABOR LEADER

César Chávez

(1927-1993)
American Civil Rights Activist

César Chávez had a dream to dedicate his life for the cause for all migrant farm workers to receive fair treatment, fair pay, and fair working conditions. He remembered that when he was young, he and his family toiled in the fields for hours under the conditions of the hot sun, no breaks, and little water.

César Chávez was the most important Latino leader in United States history. His accomplishments were so great that many looked to him as a saint and a modern-day Gandhi.

Mr. Chávez was born near Yuma, Arizona. He also served in the United States Navy from 1944 to 1946.

To bring awareness to the dangers from the pesticides to farm workers and people eating the produce, in 1968 Mr. Chávez called for a national boycott against California grape growers.

Through hunger strikes and other methods to bring attention to his cause, Mr. Chávez persuaded 17 million Americans, and millions more worldwide, to stop eating grapes.

He co-founded with Dolores Huerta the National Farm Workers Association, known today as the United Farm Workers Union (UFW).

Mr. Chávez also had a dream and goal that through hard work he could get out of poverty, send his children to college, and create a better environment for his people.

On August 8, 1994, César Chávez received the presidential Medal of Freedom. March 31st is a national holiday, César Chávez Day.

One of his quotes was:

"If you really want to make a friend, go to someone's house and eat with him... [T]he people who give you their food give you their heart."

On April 23, 1993, César Chávez died in his sleep. Many feel that his hunger strikes contributed to his death.

REACH FOR THE STARS

"SOME PEOPLE SEE THINGS AS THEY ARE AND SAY WHY. I DREAM THINGS THAT NEVER WERE AND SAY WHY NOT?"

ROBERT F. KENNEDY
1925~1968
UNITED STATES SENATOR

Robert F. Kennedy

(1925-1968) 64th United States Attorney General

One of Robert F. Kennedy's dreams for freedom is seen in his famous quote, "Some men see things as they are, and ask why. I dream of things that never were and ask why not."

Mr. Kennedy expressed his support for helping minorities and the civil rights movements.

Robert F. Kennedy was the brother of John F. Kennedy, the 35th President of the United States. Robert Kennedy was also a U.S. senator from New York. During his brother's administration, Robert Kennedy was the United States Attorney General. He was also his brother's most trusted confidant and advisor.

In 1952 Robert Kennedy was his brother's campaign manager for the United States Senate and again in 1960 for John's presidential campaign.

Mr. Kennedy served in World War II, and in 1948 he graduated from Harvard University. In 1951, he received a law degree.

To most people, Mr Kennedy was known as "Bobby." To many, he was a hero and a new hope for our country. In 1968 Mr. Kennedy ran for president of the United States and showed himself as a voice for the powerless and an advocate for human rights. He understood the plight of Dr. Martin Luther King, Jr. and César Chávez, having met with both men to share their dreams.

With his charisma, Mr. Kennedy had outstanding public praise and was highly respected for his renowned outlook on human rights and his stand against the unpopular Vietnam War.

From 1961 to 1964 as the United States attorney general, Mr. Kennedy fought against organized crime in America.

On June 5, 1968, while campaigning for the office of president of the United States and following his victory speech at the Ambassador Hotel in Los Angeles (which has since been torn down and a school is now in its place), Mr. Kennedy was assassinated. He died the next day, June 6th, at the young age of 42.

Some of quotes from Robert Kennedy are:

"Only those who dare to fail greatly can ever achieve greatly."

"We must continue to prove to the world that we can provide a rising standard of living for all men without loss of civil rights or human dignity to any man."

Abraham Lincoln

(1809-1865) 16th United States President

Abraham Lincoln's dream was to free all men, no matter what their race or nationality, and he fought for the abolishment of slavery while also trying to keep the country united. Thus, on January 1, 1963, as the 16th U.S. President, Mr. Lincoln declared that the slaves be forever free.

Mr. Lincoln is considered one of the greatest presidents this country has ever had. He started out as a lawyer.

During his now famous Gettysburg Address during the American Civil War, a time that tore this country apart, President Lincoln said, "The world will little note nor long remember what we say here, but it can never forget what they did here."

There are many incredible similarities between President Lincoln and President Kennedy. Both men were shot in the back of the head on a Friday with their wife at their side. In 1861, President Lincoln had a police superintendent whole last name was Kennedy, who worried about Lincoln's safety. In 1961, President Kennedy's secretary whose last name was Lincoln, was concerned about Kennedy's safety. Lincoln's and Kennedy's assassins were both shot to death before their trial. Lincoln's son Robert and Kennedy's son John, Jr. both lived at 3014 N Street in Georgetown (located in northwest Washington, D.C.). Lincoln and Kennedy at the time of their assassination had a vice president whose last name was Johnson, who became president. Lincoln was elected president in 1860 and Kennedy was elected president in 1960.

On April 14, 1865, President Abraham Lincoln was assassinated in Washington, D.C., watching a play at The Ford Theatre.

Some of President Lincoln's best quotes are:

"Nearly all men can stand adversity, but if you want to test a man's character, give him power."

"I think that slavery is wrong, morally socially and politically. I desire that it should be no further spread in these United States, and I should not object if it should gradually terminate in the whole Union."

"Give me six hours to chop down a tree and I will spend the first four sharpening the axe."

Ford Theatre

Sir Winston Churchill

(1874 1965)

British Prime Minister of the United Kingdom, Army Officer, Writer

Winston Churchill's dream and unyielding fight was to keep England and the rest of the free world free from Nazi Germany who was overrunning Western Europe and who had bombed and almost destroyed Britain.

Known as the "bulldog warrior" Churchill will always be remembered as the last of the great statesman, and as a person of multiple geniuses as being able to foresee future dangers that could affect his country. He was one of the first to recognize and warn others of Hitler's danger to freedom and human rights.

During World War 2, Mr. Churchill, along with America's president Roosevelt and Russia's dictator Stalin formed what was known as "the big three" to fight Hitler.

Following his grandfather who was a duke, and his father who was a British statesman, Mr. Churchill, at age 26, in 1900, went into politics becoming a member of the English Parliament, which is like America's congress. He later became prime minister, which is to England what the president is to America.

Mr. Churchill ranked eighth in his class of 150 and graduated 20th in his class of 130.

He built a supreme armed force called the Royal Navy, which was considered one of the best in the world.

As a hero of England, Mr. Churchill had fought in five wars, gave 8,000 speeches, and held nine cabinet offices.

Some of his traits were his cigar and victory sign.

In 1917, Mr. Churchill was awarded the United States Distinguished Service Medal. He was knighted by Queen Elizabeth of England and becoming Sir Winston in 1953.

Some of Winston Churchill's quotes are:

"Never, never, never give up."

"Courage is what it takes to stand up and speak; courage is also what it takes to sit down and listen."

"We make a living by what we get, but we make a life by what we give."

REACH FOR THE STARS

"A lie is not important except in the impact it has on other lives."

JACKIE ROBINSON
1919~1972
MAJOR LEAGUE BASEBALL PLAYER

Jackie Robinson

(1919-1972) American Professional Baseball Player

Jackie Robinson's dream was all about playing the game of baseball. At age 28, Jackie Robinson's inclusion into the then New York Brooklyn Dodgers as the first African American major league baseball player on April 15, 1947, brought about one of the Civil Rights Movement's most significant achievements. Adding to the Movement, he was arrested during his boot camp training in Texas for refusing to move to the back of a segregated bus where whites sat in the front and blacks had to sit in the back.

Subject to constant catcalls during his first few games, along with racial slurs being hurled at him, having to sit in the back of the public buses, reading signs in restaurants and on private homes proclaiming "No Colored," and enduring anonymous death threats, Jackie Robinson had promised that he would not fight back.

As a student at John Muir High School and Pasadena Junior College, both in Pasadena, California, Mr. Robinson was an excellent athlete and played in four sports: basketball, football, track, and baseball. Then, at the University of California, Los Angeles (UCLA), he was the school's first student to win four varsity letters in four sports. His older brother Matthew won the silver medal in the 200 meters in the 1936 Olympic Games in Berlin.

Mr. Robinson served in the United States Army as a second lieutenant during World War II from 1942 to 1944.

Jackie Robinson's awards and recognitions are numerous. For instance, after hitting 12 home runs in his first year in the majors, he was named the National League Rookie of the Year in 1947. Soon he would be named the league's Most Valuable Player in 1949, become a World Series champ in 1955, and be elected to the Baseball Hall of Fame in 1962. In 1976 his Brooklyn, New York, home was named a national historic landmark. He was posthumously awarded the Presidential Medal of Freedom by President Ronald Reagan in 1984. In 1987, the Major League Rookie of the Year Award was renamed the Jackie Robinson Award. Finally, in 2003 Mr. Robinson was recognized with the Congressional Gold Medal in Washington, D.C. by President Bush. His name is now synonymous with the desegregation and the re-definition of professional sports.

The Dodgers retired Robinson's number 42 on June 4,1972; and on April 15, 2007, Major League baseball invited players to wear Robinson's number 42 to commemorate the 60th anniversary of his debut into the league.

One of Mr. Robinson's quotes was:

"There's not an American in this country free until every one of us is free."

Thomas Jefferson

(1743-1826) 3rd United States President, Author of the Declaration of Independence

Thomas Jefferson's dream was that all people should be blessed with happiness and peace. As such, Mr. Jefferson, at the age of 33 in 1776, drafted the Declaration of Independence, which is considered one of the most powerful testaments to liberty.

In 1767, at age 24, Mr. Jefferson became a successful lawyer. He had entered college when he was sixteen, and he also established a system of free education.

Thomas Jefferson had many titles: scientist, writer, inventor, architect, and owner of more than 600 slaves. He was also minister to France, governor of Virginia, the first U.S. Secretary of State under President Washington, and the second U.S. Vice President under President John Adams before becoming our third president at age 57.

As a founding father of the United States of America, Jefferson was the founder of what became the Democratic Party. He also urged the addition of the "Bill of Rights" to our Constitution.

As president, Jefferson arranged the Louisiana Purchase, doubling the size of the United States at the time at a cost of $16 million dollars, thus adding another state to our union.

President Jefferson created and established the University of Virginia, planning the grounds and buildings, plus overseeing the whole project. He also designed his home, a mansion called Monticello, which took 35 years to build.

Lovable and likable, people called Mr. Jefferson, "Long

Tom" because he was so tall.

Among Thomas Jefferson's quotes is:

"Honesty is the first chapter in the book of wisdom."

The White House – Thomas Jefferson's Term

General Douglas MacArthur

(1880 -1964) U.S. Army General, Field Marshall for the Philippine Army, U.S. Chief of Staff

General Douglas MacArthur was one of the most honoured and respected United States five-star generals whose dream was to keep America safe from foreign enemies.

On January 26, 1880, General MacArthur was born into a strong military family. His father Arthur was an army captain who fought in the Civil War. He followed in his father's footsteps.

After graduating from high school, General MacArthur enrolled at West Point at age 19 and was the top scholar in his class in 1903. In 1919, he was the superintendent of West Point for three years, during which he was promoted to Brigadier General.

President Franklin D. Roosevelt made MacArthur his military advisor in 1935 and gave him the job of building a Philippine army. In 1942 the Japanese forced MacArthur to retreat. He promised the Philippine people he would be back and true to his promise, he did return to help the Philippine people with their freedom.

In 1945, President Harry S. Truman appointed him as the supreme allied commander of the U.S. Army. He would also in later years meet with presidents John F. Kennedy and Lyndon B. Johnson, to advise them on military matters at hand.

General MacArthur oversaw the signing of the surrender documents with Japan on board the U.S. battleship Missouri in Tokyo Bay, Japan. This effectively ended World War II. It was the first time in 2,000 years that Japan was forced to acknowledge defeat in a war.

A strong-minded military general, MacArthur criticized President Truman's handling of the Korean War. Because of this, he was relieved of his command in 1951, ending his military career. He remained a hero to the American people and others around the world.

A famous quote by General Douglas MacArthur was:

"The soldier above all others prays for peace, for it is the soldier who must bear the deepest wounds and scars of war."

Franklin D. Roosevelt

(1882-1945)
32nd President of the United States

Franklin D. Roosevelt's dream was to keep America and its people safe from all enemies who were trying to overtake America, and to keep the American people working with good jobs. He also was determined to pull America out of the Great Depression.

Mr. Roosevelt was the only United States president to win four consecutive elections. Today, a president can only serve two terms.

His uncle was Theodore "Teddy" Roosevelt, the 26th president of the United States. Like other presidents, Franklin. Roosevelt started out as a lawyer. Later, he was governor of New York for two terms after being elected to the New York state legislature at age 28.

Mr. Roosevelt was stricken with polio in 1921, which left him crippled and in need of a wheel chair. He never allowed himself to be seen using the wheelchair in public.

On October 29, 1929, America's financial backbone known as the stock market crashed (went broke), creating the Great Depression. That day became known as "Black Tuesday," when people lost everything: all their money, homes, and jobs.

Within months of becoming president in 1932, Roosevelt saw that he had to do something, and so he created many social programs with his "New Deal" initiative to bring the country back on its feet. On August 14, 1935, President Roosevelt signed into law the Social Security Act. It was designed to pay a monthly income to retired works ages 62 and older. More than 80 years later, millions of Americans receive Social Security payments. Hopefully, it will continue in the future.

On December 7, 1941, when Japan almost destroyed America's Pacific naval fleet at Pearl Harbor, Mr. Roosevelt famously proclaimed it "a date which will live in infamy."

For Americans, Mr. Roosevelt was portrayed as a man for, and of, the people. He was America's hero.

Franklin D. Roosevelt's Desk in the White House

George Washington

(1732-1799)
1st President on the United States, a U.S. Founding Father

George Washington's dream was to free the United States from the rule of England. As a military general, Washington led the American troops to victory against the mighty British in the War of Independence, which lasted six years.

At the age of 23, George Washington was made the commander of the Virginia troops, and in 1775 he was nominated by future president John Adams to be the commander of the Army for the "Defense of American Liberty."

George Washington was known as "General of the army" and president of all the people. In his day, he was a churchwarden (overseer of church affairs), tobacco planter, land broker, speculator, and surveyor.

Washington became a wealthy landowner, thanks to his marriage to Martha which brought in an 18,000-acre estate, along with land he received from his military service. He raised horses and cattle and had a fruit orchard. At one point, because it was legal, he owned more than 300 slaves. The capital of the United States when Mr. Washington was president was New York City.

George Washington was elected the first president of the United States on February 4, 1789 at the age of 57. As the first president of this young country, he had to set an example for future generations of presidents. His first cabinet included future presidents, John Adams and Thomas Jefferson.

In 1787 he became chairman of the constitutional convention that in 1788 approved the Constitution of the United States. Before the term "Mr. President" was agreed on, terms such as "His Elective Majesty," "His Highness," and "His Elective Highness," were debated. It was President Washington himself who selected "Mr. President."

George Washington's Mt Vernon Museum and Education Center

REACH FOR THE STARS

"MR. GORBACHEV, TEAR DOWN THIS WALL!"

RONALD REAGAN
1911~2004
40th PRESIDENT OF THE UNITED STATES

Ronald Reagan

(1911-2004)
40th President of the United States, State Governor, Actor

Ronald Reagan's dream was to always keep America safe, secure, and protected from missiles from other countries that wanted to harm the United States, and to reduce nuclear missiles, which he did with the Soviet Union.

Mr. Reagan was the first professional actor to become a United States president, and at age 69 was the oldest person elected to the country's highest office.

Ronald Reagan had many roles in his life, starting out as a lifeguard and a radio announcer in Illinois. He acted in more than 53 films and television shows and served as president of the Screen Actors Guild (the actors' union) from 1947 to 1952 and again from 1959 to 1960. Mr. Reagan's nickname was "The Gripper" after a movie role in 1940 where he played the Notre Dame Football star, George Gipp.

Mr. Reagan was a captain when he served in the United States Army.

On March 30, 1981, after just two months during his first term as president, an assassination attempt struck him with a bullet, narrowly missing his heart. Afterward, he said to his wife Nancy, "Honey, I forgot to duck."

Mr. Reagan started his political career in high school, as student body president and went on to be student council president in college. He entered professional politics in 1966, being elected to two terms as governor of California from 1966 to 1974 before serving two terms as president from 1980 to 1988.

In 1991, the Ronald Reagan Presidential Museum opened in Simi Valley, California. After his death, Mr. Reagan was buried on the grounds of the museum.

According to a USA Today/Gallup Poll, President Ronald Reagan is considered one of the best and most respected presidents this country has ever had.

Ronald Reagan Presidential Museum

REACH FOR THE STARS

"THE WORLD AS I SEE IT."

I WANT TO KNOW HOW GOD CREATED THIS WORLD."

ALBERT EINSTEIN
1879~1955
PHYSICIST

Albert Einstein

(1879 – 1955) Physicist

Albert Einstein had a dream to learn how the world and the universe were created. He struggled to find the laws of physics, bringing about his theory of relativity, the force of gravity, and dealing with space and time.

Tutored by a family friend in philosophy and higher mathematics, which opened doors for him in his future. He was independently studying mathematics and science by the age of 12, and at 23 he was concentrating on the task of matter and energy.

Mr. Einstein was astonished at the forces that turned the needle on a compass, which started his interest in being a physicist at five years old. When he was 12, he read a geometry book over and over, and wrote his first science paper at sixteen based on a thought he had as to what a light beam would look like if you ran alongside it at the same speed. This would make the light beam seem frozen and not moving, when in fact the light beam is moving. That's an example of how his brain worked.

He discovered that the speed of light remained constant, and that tiny particles of matter could be converted into large amounts of energy. In the 1920s, while he was in his 30s, Einstein predicted that the universe is always contracting and expanding. This theory has since been proven.

When Mr. Einstein formulated the theory of relativity, he predicted the effect that when a ray of light passes near a massive body, the ray of light should bend. This prediction led to his subsequent prediction that starlight passing near the sun should be slightly deflected by gravity. Yet again, he was right.

In 1921, Mr. Einstein was awarded the Nobel Prize for physics in 1921.

The most famous equation of science, $E=mc^2$, was Mr. Einstein's theory which he developed when he was 26. It would in later years put him behind the creation of the atom bomb, which is one of the most important events in modern history. After learning that the Germans planned to develop an atomic bomb, Einstein wrote a letter to U.S. President Roosevelt suggesting to perhaps use an atomic bomb on Japan. The rest is history.

On April 17, 1955, Mr. Einstein was rushed to a hospital where he refused surgery, saying, "I want to go when I want. It is tasteless to prolong life artificially. I have done my share, it is time to go. I will do it elegantly." He died the next day and his brain was removed and is now at the Princeton University Medical Center for doctors of neuroscience to study.

Other noteworthy quotes from Albert Einstein are:

"Not everything that can be counted counts, and not everything that counts can be counted."

"Everybody is a genius. But if you judge a fish by its ability to climb a tree, it will live its whole life believing that it is stupid."

"There are only two ways to live your life. One is as though nothing is a miracle. The other is as though everything is a miracle."

REACH FOR THE STARS

"NOTHING CAN BE SAID TO BE CERTAIN, EXCEPT DEATH AND TAXES."

BENJAMIN FRANKLIN
1706~1790
STATESMAN

Benjamin Franklin

(1706-1790) Founding Father of the United States, Scientist

Benjamin Franklin's dream was to help build America as a great country. He is considered one of America's greatest minds and is best known as one of the founding fathers of the United States of America.

Mr. Franklin was many things in his lifetime. He was a scientist, inventor, statesman, printer, philosopher, musician, and economist. He was the first United States Ambassador to France and helped elect George Washington as our first president. Also, he started the first fire department and the first professional police force in 1736.

By trade Mr. Franklin was a printer. However, by fame he was a scientist. In 1728, he opened his own printing business and became publisher of a newspaper. He published the "Poor Richard's Almanac" from 1732 to 1758.

Mr. Franklin invented the bifocal glasses, the Franklin stove (still in use today), the odometer, and the lightning rod. He started his electrical experiment in 1752, drawing electricity from a cloud through a kite string with a key on it. Today the lightning rod is used to protect people, buildings, and ships from lightning. He also invented swim fins, was the first to propose the idea of daylight savings time, set up the first fire insurance company, and made the first political cartoon.

Mr. Franklin earned honorary degrees from Oxford, Harvard, and Yale universities because of his brilliance of being self-educated.

As one of the founding fathers of the United States, Mr. Franklin was a signer on the Declaration of Independence of 1776. He also had the distinction of being known as the spokesman for America. His picture is still on our $100 bill.

Mr. Franklin was one of the first people to think in terms of one nation rather than separate colonies. In 1790 he petitioned Congress to abolish slavery.

Some of Mr. Franklin's famous quotes, most of which are still used in regular discourse today, are:

"Haste makes waste."

"God helps them that help themselves."

"A penny saved is a penny earned."

"Remember, time is money."

"An apple a day keeps the doctor away."

"We are all born ignorant, but one must work hard to remain stupid."

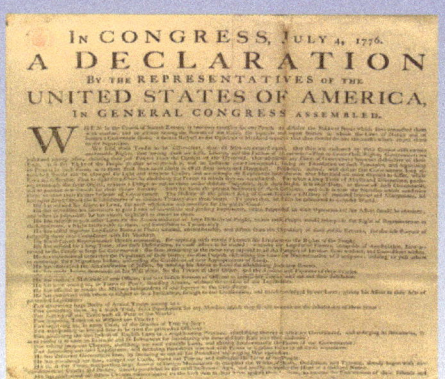

Mohandas Gandhi

(1869-1948)
Indian Activist

Mohandas Gandhi had a dream and a passion for nonviolence for the people of India. Gandhi, as he is and was known, lived a self-sacrificing life. He did however start out as a lawyer in 1893, studying in London, England. As it turned out, this was not to be his calling. One reason was because he was too shy. Much like Martin Luther King, Jr. and Mother Teresa, he was a believer for the rights of the poor and oppressed.

Ghandi committed himself to a life of purity by practicing celibacy, doing manual labor, self-reliance on everything he needed, and even fasting. He was a vegetarian, eating only fruit, raw and cooked vegetables, and dates. He never ate meat, fish or eggs and never had team coffee or any kind of alcohol.

He experienced racial prejudice when he was forced from a train because a white man objected to his being on the same train even though Gandhi had a first-class ticket.

Gandhi was one of the most influential, spiritual, and political leaders of his time. He worked hard to alleviate discrimination and poverty, and to liberate women. For this he was put in jail for two years.

He started a new community where people living there had to be nonviolent and truthful. They had to do their own farming for a living and make their own clothes. Also, they could have no servants or personal possessions, and women enjoyed their freedom and had equal rights the same as men.

Gandhi continued to fight for independence for India from under the British rule by boycotting British products and businesses.

During his time, he was the most important person in India. He was considered the father of his country and its people and was called "Mahatma," which means "great soul," as like a saint.

Mohandas Gandhi was on the cover of Time Magazine, an American weekly news magazine, on March 31, 1930, January 5, 1931, the year he was named the publication's Man of the Year, and again on June 30, 1947.

Sadly, like many famous people in this book, Gandhi was assassinated on January 30, 1948, in Delhi, India.

My Dream

My name is _____

My Dream is _____

_____

_____

_____

_____

_____

_____

_____

_____

_____

_____

_____   _____

Signature   Date

About the Author

Ken Dean started his career as an actor in Chicago, during a road show of the musical, **West Side Story**. He has been a resident of Canyon Country, California since 1981 and is one of the founding fathers of the City of Santa Clarita, California.

Ken developed a love for writing children's books and has written ten to date. He has always had a fascination with animals and insects which has led him to write children's books about them. Each book has a message for kids, a happy ending, and a likable protagonist. They feature compelling characters in a believable world, a kid's world.

After three years of research, Ken completed his own children's history book, titled, **Reach For The Stars**. It is written for children ages 7 to 12 providing biographical and historical background with essential quotes from each person to illustrate his or her thinking, philosophy, and impact on the world.

Ken is an award-winning interior designer and has been teaching in the William S. Hart School District for seventeen years and the Burbank School District for two. He is also a set designer.

www.ingramcontent.com/pod-product-compliance
Lightning Source LLC
Chambersburg PA
CBHW042356280426
43661CB00095B/1131